To Kirsten,

Purrpetuate Pawsitivity!

— Tasha Bock

Feminist Felines Copyright © 2015 Tasha Bock.
All Rights Reserved by Tasha Bock
This book or any portion thereof may not be reproduced or used in any manner whatsoever
without the express written permission of the publisher except for the use of brief quotations in a book review.

Published by Tasha Bock
For order or press inquiries visit:
www.feministfelines.com
(760) 815-0156

Library of Congress Control Number: 2015911770
ISBN 978-0-9963616-0-6

1. Children's 2. Novelty 3. Gender 4. Contemporary Issues
First Edition and Printing, 2015
Printed in PRC
10 9 8 7 6 5 4 3 2 1

For my Dad
who taught my sister & me that no dream is too big

Once upon 2015, there were two cats, Mischief and Tinker. These were not two ordinary cats, these were fierce and feisty... feminist felines!

You see, Mischief and Tinker believed that all cats, no matter girl or boy, deserved equal rights. Opportunities such as going to school or **purrsuing** any career they chose to **chase**.

The cats realized that the best way to contribute to feline feminism was to put one paw in front of the other and lead by example. Instead of **mewing** and **hissing**, they focused on leading by doing.

Each of their decisions and choices built up to make them strong cats…

Tinker didn't let the **pawtriarchy** define her body image. She ate what and when she wanted to.

She embraced her curves but kept healthy through a rigorous fitness regimen and playing games.

Her favorite? Running and **purrsuing** a string!

Mischief wasn't afraid to show her intelligence and never dumbed herself down. She realized early that all the **cool cats** weren't afraid to show their smarts. She resented being called bossy and controlling just because she had a strong will and assertive behavior.

She **purrfered** more intellectual games that involved problem solving, such as retrieving precariously positioned toys!

The two cats began proclaiming themselves feminist felines after an enlightening day out on the town.......

That fateful day, they had decided to head uptown for some fun. They hailed a cab and the taxi **whiskered** them along 5th Avenue, past the fancy shops, alongside Central Park and then to Museum Mile.

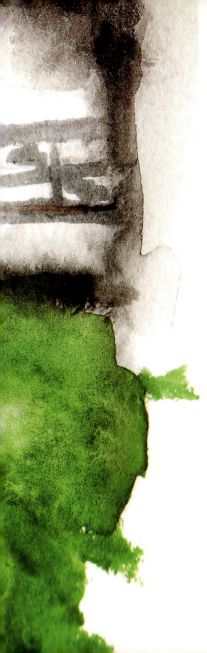

They **bounded** up the steps of a large and imposing art museum.

"I want to go to the Renaissance gallery," proclaimed Mischief.

"No, let's go to the sculpture gallery," sulked Tinker.

"No **knead** to be a **sourpuss**, we can do both!" responded Mischief. "We will actually be better off by compromising and working together."

"You are **litterally** always right," Tinker replied, visibly brightened.

They arrived in a long room of paintings depicting biblical scenes and meandered down the corridor, passing a large picture of a lion and a lamb lying next to each other peacefully. They stopped in front of a picture of Noah's Ark. All sorts of animals were filing into the boat in pairs.

"Look, Mischief—the girl animals are walking behind the boys—why aren't they walking together, next to one another?" queried Tinker.

"Throughout **hisstory**, girls haven't always been treated with the same respect and rights that we are accustomed to today. In fact, in many ways and in many places, girls and boys are still not equal," replied Mischief.

"**Fur** real?" asked Tinker, wide eyed. "You have **gato** be **kitten** me!"

"Its true," Mischief said, solemnly shaking her head. "In little ways and in big! We live in one of the most progressive countries… Imagine what it's like for kittens around the world who can't play and learn as they wish! Lots of other female felines are denied an education and a way to support themselves! And those who have jobs are often paid less than their male coworkers of the same **pedigree**!"

"That can't stand—I don't want to wait for my **ninth life** to do something…. I want to be part of change now!" intoned Tinker.

"Well, some say that we've broken through the glass ceiling but I think we are still **cats on a hot tin roof**..... Gaining your footing is hard when you can't comfortably stand on your own four paws! It's enough to make me **hissterical**," expounded Mischief.

"Yes, it really is a **catastrophy**," agreed Tinker solemnly. But, with a resolute set to her jaw, she stated. "I am going to work on **grooming** myself in all facets of my life and **pouncing** on every opportunity, **beclaws** I can make a difference."

The two linked tails and strolled **further** into the museum, united in their quest to create a future where all felines would be empowered to follow their dreams. "I'm **pawsitive** we can make a difference and **prospurr** if we support one another," vowed Mischief.

"Yes—and let's start **here and meow**," pledged Tinker.

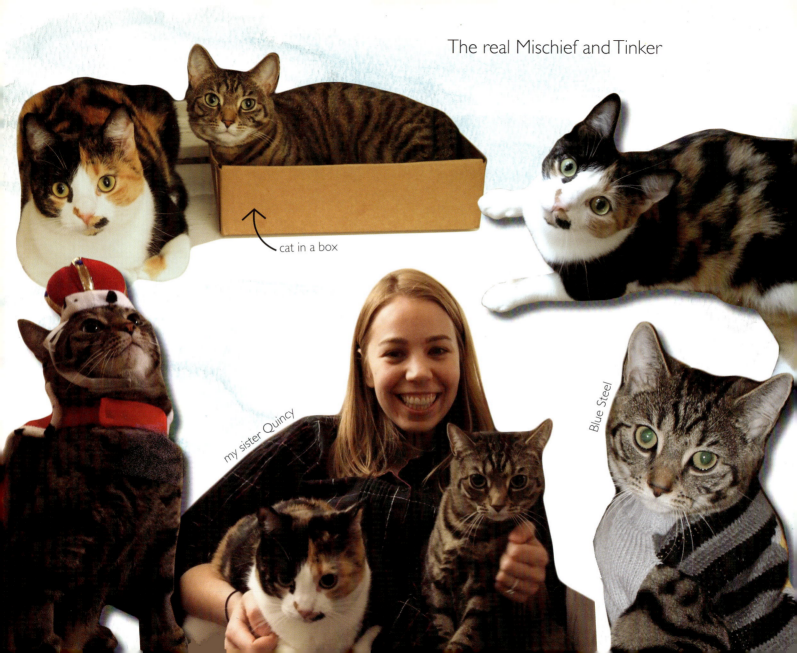

Inspiration

Mischief and Tinker were both adopted from New York City animal shelters by my older sister Quincy and are the protagonists of this story. Their distinct and determined personalities are reflected in this *tail*. Quincy taught me the importance of feminism. A feminist is anyone who believes that girls and boys deserve the same rights and treatment. Many leading thinkers emphasize that equality for women—at school, in the workplace, and elsewhere—will be instrumental in eradicating many of humanity's greatest problems. It's in the best interest of all of us to support one another!

About the Author

Tasha is a fifth-generation Californian. Her roots are in San Diego but she has been fortunate to travel, study and work around the world. She graduated from Dartmouth College in 2015. She loves horseback riding, the ocean, carrot cake, jewelry design, adventures and her family.

sharp, happy, exuberant, faithful, intrepid, funny, elegant, strong, clever, humble, consistent, inventive, encouraging, brave, resourceful, daring, purrseverant, valiant, steadfast, adept, caring, compassionate, spirited, resilient, plucky, litterate, honest, smart, adventurous, pawlite, loyal, appreciative, entrepreneurial, dogged, honest, wise, sincere, graceful, charming, radiant, proactive, candid, confident, curious, generous, loving, focused, buoyant, savvy, canny, poppurrlar, quirky, fine, gracious, trustworthy, determined, poised, purrposeful, bold, brainy, capable, inquisitive, assertive, pawsitive, assured, articulate, snazzy, fantabbyulous, bright, gung-ho, determined, outgoing, cool, enterprising, creative, imaginative, charming, kind, passionate, resolute, helpful, uplifting, effurvescent, lively, courageous, incandescent, heroic, gracious, exuberant, unstoppable, earnest, charismatic, accountable, sagacious, crafty, responsible, considerate, tenacious, talented, genuine, inspiring, dependable, ingenious, accountable, intuitive, committed, disciplined, wily, thoughtful, industrious